THE PHILOSOPHER'S
WINDOW

For Nora all [ecnon]

At Purdue

Nov. 2 '95

Also by Allen Grossman

Allen Grossman

THE PHILOSOPHER'S

WINDOW

and Other Poems

A NEW DIRECTIONS BOOK

ACKNOWLEDGMENTS
"The Great Work Farm Elegy" first appeared in *Colorado Review* and was included in *The Best American Poetry 1993*, edited by Louise Glück and David Lehman (Scribners). "The Snowfall" was originally published in *The American Poetry Review*.

The illustrations on page 12 are from *The Great Iron Ship*, by James Dugan (London: Hamish Hamilton, 1953).

Manufactured in the United States of America
New Directions Books are published on acid-free paper.
First published as New Directions Paperbook 807 in 1995
Published simultaneously in Canada by Penguin Books Canada Limited

Library of Congress Cataloging-in-Publication Data

Grossman, Allen R., 1932–
    The philosopher's window: a romance and other poems / Allen Grossman.
        p.   cm.
    ISBN 0-8112-1300-5
    I. Title.
PS3557.R67P45 1995
811'.54—dc20   95-6257
                                                                    CIP

New Directions Books are published for James Laughlin
by New Directions Publishing Corporation
80 Eighth Avenue, New York 10011

The Philosopher's Window
is presented to Judith Grossman

Recevons tous les influx de vigueur et de tendresse
réelle. Et à l'aurore, armés d'une ardente patience,
nous entrerons aux splendides villes.

Rimbaud

Contents

THE POEMS in this book tell one story with a beginning, a middle, and an end. The first poem, "The Great Work Farm Elegy," is the beginning. The long romance of "The Philosopher's Window" is the middle. There are several endings.

The voice, throughout the book, is the voice of an old man compelled by the insistent questioning of the children to *explain* himself. On the long journey of his life, as he remembers it, everything speaks (which is only just) and teaches him by speaking to him (which is sheer good luck).

This old man tells how, as a boy, he became a bird, a ship's parrot, the world's poet (who also appears in the poem as a man or woman endlessly climbing the poet's stair—short of breath as usual). He tells how he was wrecked against the Gates of Night (the end of thought). How he was consoled by the entertainment on shipboard (particularly the aerialists, contortionists, and jugglers). And how he found companionship with a sailor and a swineherd (until they disappeared). At last, he sees the sun go down (like fire in the mind) over a western ocean.

The philosopher (who has a toothache) watches all this from his window, dreams of reality ("The Snowfall"), and pronounces the rules by which the world must be made every morning ("Whoever Builds"). These rules the philosopher learned from the poet who learned them by laborious stealth —*the poet's great work*—from the God.

At last, the old man wakes in stormy June ("June, June") when the lilacs are gone.

One

THE GREAT WORK

FARM ELEGY

The Great Work Farm Elegy

1.

In Adam's house, in Paradise, the room is still.
The hours, equal. The windows, open to the air.
The floor is swept. The flowers, real. The light
Is far *and* near—like water, very very clear
As it was in the beginning of the hours:
Before the bay of the world did empty out
Its light into the sea of light. And from the shore
The sea withdrew afar, and gathered up, and towered;
And night descended gradual and great with all its fires,
And at the door pale death knocked with his foot . . . .

2.

All night, seated beneath the willows you know of,
On every watermeadow in the universe, we write
The long letters of mind by the light of the moon.
But now day breaks, and a million suns say:
"Send it!" —And I (for one) reply: "To whom?
To the townsfolk of New Ulm? Or the Great Bog of Cloon?"
"No!", says the one sun that sees me. "Send it
To your own whom you dare not name! To her,
The loon on the lake; to him, at the shore: the countenance
In the abyss —with copies to your death, etc."

3.

Why not say it? You blue-eyed infant souls!
I am here to tell you on this shaken earth:
Our face and the form of our bodies, are not
Known to us. And the elevation of the golden house
We build is unknown to us. And the gods of the house,
That stand inside, are, as I have said elsewhere,
Enraged. Judgement has not yet been passed, nor
The sentence written, nor the harvest carried home:
But the fields are white with the risen grain.
And witnesses clamor in the porch and on the stair

4.

And crowd the threshold, where they pause—some still
In the open air, under the raking light,
Their harbinger that chalks the door. Is it
A dream, householders? Oh no! The children have
Come home out of the air, like rain and snow.
For what, then, do we build this house and keep it
But for the children? —Now, as at all times,
I hear them. *Now*, I see their painted clothes.
And the room darkens and ignites, as the clouds
Slake and re-illume the low light of the dawn.

5.

One says, "Old man! You lectured in my dreams,
And uttered words I did not understand. *Either*
You did not speak clearly, as often you do not;
Or I did not pay attention. (Often I don't.) So!
We have come to give you *another chance*. Explain
Again what you said in my dream. What did you
Say? What did you *mean*? What?" —Now, more than ever,
I hear them at my door, laughing and talking
Among themselves, and putting their question
Under the raking light, on the shore of the sky.

6.

—*I will explain*: "The earth is mourning (*'Toha!'*)
And crying (*'Boha!'*), because her lot is evil."
"Know this!" (I say). "The earth is broken, creased,
Scratched, crazed, pitted, torn, always in motion,
Ribbed, rock-ribbed, wrinkled as the skin of
A starving animal and scarred—or radiant
Like the body of a woman who arose to bathe,
And then lay down again to rest and consider.
And the air is never still for all the vows
(*'Love of my life,'* etc.), and the switching of engines.

7.

"And I make no difference for mind, that 'ocean.'
What, then, does it mean to begin again, *dilectissimi*,
As if from the beginning? It means just this:
To be penetrated by a dark myth—in order
To leave it empty at your death, like a book
Forgotten on the asphalt that becomes, thereby,
The one dark book which makes good sense. The wind
Opens it. And the rains of a long summer
Evening erase the pages, and the very page.
And there it lies, a ruin. And is never found.

8.

"And the woman says—the one, you will remember,
Who lay down again to consider: 'The light
Has betrayed me, the low light of the dawn.'
'Darken the room,' she says. 'Write me no more letters,
Under the willows by the light of the moon.'
—So I tell her the story of the great work
In the beginning: how under the willows
On all the watermeadows of the universe
Our hand began the long letters of mind
For her, with copies to our death, etc. . . . .

9.

" 'Then as now' (I say) 'the Rider was on high,
Killing and quickening, as it is written,
Sowing and reaping, and feeding the rain
That rots the stack.' " ("What!" the children cry. "Say
What?" "Look up!" is my reply. "It's clear as day,
Dilectissimi.") —"There was a farmer, Hermann;
His wife, Irene; and I was the boy. Late summer.
The bales lay in the field. And time that is
Destroying me appeared to me in the low light,
Awaking the thirty dogs of the farm

10.

"(Old and young, lame skeletons and firm-fleshed,
Farting hounds) to the hunt that followed on
Among the bales, across the stubble fields
Of timothy (a grass that loves the marshes,
A running root), behind the Rider of the Sky,
Gigantic form. The earth, with all its scars,
Lay open to the eye—the harvest of the hay.
And a cloud that shone like a hammered rail
Overhung the river, far to the north,
Toward which the farmer drove us in his Plymouth

11.

"Automobile—like a bat out of hell.
In the neighbor farm, at the river's edge,
A birthday was going on—an overheated
Kitchen, strange animals, and the *Weiberdeutsch*
(Dreary language of carnal origin),
The wisdom of the women of New Ulm.
And strange! Strange to tell! Over the lawn, I saw
A white moon, and the moon's shine, bright and thin.
'A prodigy!' sang the women of New Ulm.

12.

"—'The hay,' the farmer whispered. 'The hay will come
To harm.' Then back we went, from north to south,
Returning home at noon, like a whizzing bat,
In the Plymouth ('38) which he drove flat out.
Such was the beginning of the great work
And the dark myth (of which I spoke)—the lost
Book the wind opens, and the rains of long summer
Evenings, pouring down, erase: all the pages,
And the very page (as the heart of a man
Is emptied at the moment of his death);

13.

"And it becomes—the very page—a memory
Of memories to be, or not to be,
Remembered; and of the dreams of love unknown,
The dream. And of the work without a name,
In a nation undiscovered and its wars,
The distant glory and the murmured fame.
Thus begins, *dilectissimi*, the extreme
Poem of the wind and rain, long letter of mind
Addressed to the abyss—*and sent*: how it was
When there were two of us on earth alone,

14.

"A man, a boy, and a thousand bales of timothy
(A grass that loves old pastures, a running root
Knotted in wires by machines)—each 90
Pounds for sure, or more when it's wet.
—The Rider of the Sky led on the hunt
Followed by the thirty storm hounds of the *Great
Work Farm*, each dog with its note, each under each
Intent upon his lesson: —like didactic angels
Out of the fountains of Maimonides,
Each hound with its own harsh bell. From noon

15.

"Until the afternoon, from afternoon until
The dark the farmer of earth threw up a thousand
Bails of timothy onto the rig. I drove;
And from the rick, allegory of the work,
We built—Hermann and I—the golden house
Of the stack that kept the hay from harm.
All day above our heads the Rider of the Sky
Pursued the Scorpion, the Bison, and the Dragon Fly
Until the hay was in and the rain came down.
Then the thirty hounds of the farm (in chorus) sang

16.

"'The Song of the Constant Nymph,' and the heavens rang:
'Which are the hours of greatest simplicity?
Are they among the hours of the day:
The morning hours, for example, witness of children
In the raking light? Or are they the hours of the sun
At noon, a little before, or a little after
The meridian which says, "Behold! The general meadow!"
Or are they among the evening hours, crepuscular,
That await pale death, the guest with the swift kick,
The same at every door. —Which are the hours

17.

"'Of greatest simplicity? Are they among
The first watches of the night, the teaching powers,
When the tides of light withdraw from shore—far off,
Far out—and from the distant beacons and the towers
Difference and the dark, histories of light,
Instruct the heart. —Which are the hours of greatest
Simplicity? Are they planted among the midnight
Hours when the earth stands like a statue in
The general meadow—a statue in winter
Like a woman in time without a sister

18.

"'Who has stopped for a moment on a winter hill,
Without past or future, the same in every season,
Dark Niobe of the lovely lovely tresses,
Without a reason. —Which are the hours of
Greatest simplicity? Are they, perhaps, among
The darkest hours of the night when the monks
Begin their chant: "Or has the sight of the sun
In its glory," they sing, "Or the glow of the moon
As it walks the sky, secretly stolen my heart
Away so that I blew them a kiss . . . ?"'

19.

"Then the Rider of the Sky—the master of
The Scorpion, and Dragon Fly—answered his hounds
And sang this conclusion: 'These are the hours
Of greatest simplicity: *the hours before dawn—*
When the earth has risen from consideration
After her bath, and walks abroad alone
Conferring honor where it's due—among
The sleeping flowers in the garden. And the children
In their painted clothes, living and dead,
Crowd the doorway (the dead ones are in blue)

20.

"'Putting their questions.' 'All honor,' says the earth
'To our brightest flower, the noblest of the family,
The one who *knew the work*—and now stands here
(*Toha*) in blue.' 'Who is the Rider of the Sky?'
The dead one asks. '*Who is that masked man?'*—'I am
The truth of the messenger' (was his reply),
'Not this word or that one ("long letters of mind")
But a short scroll under the tongue signifying
The whole breath: past, passing, and to come . . .
—And I am of water the iron fountain,

21.

"'*Dilectissimi*, which explodes at the punctual
Moment of any dawn, multiplying the sun;
And the water, overflowing from that hour
Into the gravity and then the grave of time,
Becomes our truth . . . this lovely one.
—And I am the dark myth emptied at your death,
Dilectissimi, which other children find
On rainy evenings: an object lesson to
Keep them kind, like the gallows and the gibbet
And the executioner—good at ending.'"

Two

THE PHILOSOPHER'S

WINDOW

The *Great Eastern*, launched.

Isambard Kingdom Brunel.

The Philosopher's Window

(A Romance)

Mais, ô mon coeur, entends le chant des matelots!
Mallarmé

WHEN ON HIGH the heaven and earth were finished,
The moon the sun and all the stars, light enters
A room. It is time to begin the work.
The gods are done with it; but everything
Is left to do. —A woman is pretending
To read a book. The lamp beside her chair
Continues to burn, although it is day.
Upon the floor, to the left of the fireplace,
Rests a pillar of light inscribed on the wall
By a source behind me. In front of it
Stands a boy, dressed to go out, with something
In hand. A key? A paper? I don't know what . . .
—*Listen, O my heart. How the sailors sing!*

I.

THE LABYRINTH

1.

It came to pass at midnight. —Once more
The sun, which never rests, is dark. The heavens
Thunder over Jerusalem. The farmer wakes.
He looks up at the moon and stars. "This sky,"
He says out loud, "means trouble." Then the engine
Of the sun is heard dragging an iron ship
Toward dawn. The wind rises. With flail and sieve
The farmer begins to separate the seed.
"This will die," he says. "This one will not live."

2.

—Everywhere on earth are graves. The earth
Itself is of that kind. The rocks, also,
Are graves, the forests, and deserts of sand,
And pleasure-groves where we arrive after long
Walks across the flowery meadow hand in hand,
Or through the fields of ripening corn and rye
To the cliff edge when the weather is good.
And mighty ocean is a grave, and also
The shore of ocean where is a monument—

3.

Of which it is our duty to discourse,
Both night and day. Not, that is to say,
By day alone, but in the night as well;
And not in the night merely, but punctually
At the darkest hour of the night, the hour
Before the dawn when comes to mind in white
—(Can it be even a dream, O my heart?)—
The Constant Nymph, bearing this white demand:
"On pain of death (or life), YOU SING ME SOMETHING."

14

4.

But whether I come by the desert path
Or the meadow way, or through the cornfield
Or the mellowing rye, to the ocean's edge,
I have nothing to say to the Constant Nymph.
I do not have her page. *I cannot find it.*
(The mortal duty of profound discourse
Is lost to me. This monument, my grave.)
—"Then, we must take another road (why not?),"
She whispers. *"The long way round* this time—by boat."

5.

Except for me, everything speaks—even the graves.
"You will depart this shore (they say), these flowery
Beaches, a key in hand, or perhaps a stone
(What *is* it? What?), in order to arrive
Again, after long wandering, at these
Same flowery beeches. And we do not know
What the ocean says—(of the great fetch
Of the storm wave of the world we are no
More than the ensuing dust). *But it says much."*

6.

Hear then the gathered doggerel of ocean.
(—If it is the voice of a man or woman
Alone, it cannot be human—a tale
Unwritable, unwritten, written nonetheless,
But lost or never possessed. And if it is
The voice of the god alone, then it is
A storm far out in ocean—unsurvivable by ships.
But it is, after all, the sailors' long
Working of the water into song, a grand sail.)

7.

"*Awk*! This is my testament. I go by boat."—
Thus the last speaker of the extreme language:
A sulphur-headed, Antipodean parrot
Who considers himself a poet. "Awk! I go
By boat! *Let those who love me follow me!*"
—Silence falls and snow, even in this room.
Come to the darkling window, O my heart.
At whatever window the philosopher looks out,
That window becomes the philosopher's window.

II.

AT BRISTOL

8.

From where we are, high up above the gorge,
We see far off, to north and west, the ocean.
—On the ocean are wonders, island after island.
There lies thought. And after thought, at the horizon,
The end of thought. And then, beyond the end
As we look back, knowledge of the end. And when
Still thoughtful, hand in hand, we turn our eyes
Pensive, and look as the poet says, "one way,"
Before us there is neither land nor sea . . .

9.

Think then! The ocean is a restless sleeper
On its bed of stone. The turning waters sleep,
Like mind—alone. And the storms that are on ocean,
Ignorance and passion, repeat her lesson:
"Who is this pilgrim on my belly?" "What is
This burden on my bone?" —Mists of evening
Shroud the gorge. And from those mists, the roar
Of a great work: the action of the key
In a lock, and the opening of the door.

10.

Bright bird, the world is gone. *Be patient.* Patience
Is forever kind and suffers long,
And patience brings all things that are to mind:
Patience—before all worlds invisible
And visible—the unexhaustible element.
At the beginning was eternal silence.
Thereafter shouting, distant and prolonged.
Then bells, for it is Sunday. At last,
Descent of arrows, beam upon shining beam.

11.

The philosopher has a toothache. Nonetheless,
He opens for us the wonder closet of
His perpetual study with a key!
And there repose the secrets, each at rest,
Like a locked heart with crossed feet. There too,
Instruments of music. And at the breast
—Secret of secrets—the child of the kiss
Dreaming of a landscape, as of a mother.
(*And over all, absurd, the loud poetic bird.*)

12.

Behold! Everything moves. The world is like
A citizen who has ceased to believe
In "reasons of state." The evening air serene
Is full of living beings, winged and unwinged.
And justice appears at last! —Lighter than air
The big balloons flame out. The raptured neighbors
Go up and down, harmless. Harmless across
The slates, the gorge ("romantic chasm"), the desolate
Moor, the distant hills, the warrior burials.

13.

—*Who is at work?* Who? Who climbs laboriously
Upon the stair, one step and then another one?
And who is short of breath, and shorter . . . ? Who now
To the top has come: the *camera obscura*
Of our death? Who through the evening air
Looks down from the tower with the winding stair?
"What is? What has he found?" —The poet sees
The branches moving in the silent wind;
The bridge; the silent lovers among the *tumuli,*

14.

And sees the nobles, the keeper of the pleas
(In fact, the coroner), the sheriff of the shire;
The knights, the ladies, and the justice of the peace;
The king's Ukrainian torturers, and the king
Assemble, whispering among themselves,
To christen the *Great Eastern*, ship of prophecy
(Their lips move still): an iron boat, propelled
By sail *and* steam, the largest in the world.
"Awk," says the parrot, "Fecit Isambard Brunel."

III.

LAUNCHING THE *GREAT EASTERN*

15.

Low—motionless, or very slow—is the utter
Cold of the world: our mortal winter.
Within that winter is terrestrial night.
Within the winter night is winter fog,
Bitter and implacable, obscuring the dead
Weight of the iron boat, which is like thought.
The cradle screams; the big chains crack, and break.
Brunel, the Master of the Work, draws down
The hull with hooks, sidewise, into the Thames.

16.

This happened after midnight—in the dark
Before the dawn. Therefore, by night and day
And in our time, we speak of the great weight.
By night and day we stoke the furnace hole
And haul the sheet; and thereby do the work
That moves the hull. O heavy is the thought
We think, the men and women, beasts, and elements
That speak and do not speak—the acrobats
In the rigging, and elephants on deck.

17.

And far away, and on the farthest hill,
The Constant Nymph, surveying sea and land,
Sings to the wind, "I have no friend." —This is
My testament: these adventures of a Professor
Of Felicity, without his wife. In brief,
What happened to him on the maiden voyage
Of the ship of prophecy, whose destination
Was the Tree of Life. —Listen. There! The sound
Of bells, for it is Sunday. And here comes ocean . . .

18.

Ocean divine! With monsters at your heart,
And also an insomniac obsession
With lunar repetition. Ocean! Metropolis
Of flowing avenues on which the oarsman
In his boat prevails by patient renewal
Of the stroke. Ocean! The holiest grail
Of the swimmer, to whom *the demand of being
Comes suddenly home* and death is at the bottom
Of the cup. —But at the lip the man finds Paradise.

19.

For ocean is the farm of the great work.
Beneath a water oak, the Tree of Life,
Arise the fountains of the stars. From them
Descend the clearest lights—the sun and moon.
O swimmer, in the eye of the great stream!
To be seen by ocean is to be known
Without possibility of mistake, and raked
As by a hurricane, lifted up—and thrown
On rock, among the pelicans, a wreck.

20.

In the gorge of Avon the rain falls down;
And the Vedic frogs are singing, like brahmins
Practicing a vow, panegyrics of the rain.
One lows like a cow. One bleats like a goat.
One is speckled. One is yellow. In many
Ways they adorn their voices to celebrate
That day of the year: "O Master, if you
Fail you will soon return. If you succeed,
Years may pass before we meet again . . ."

21.

—The philosopher rises, who has been staring
At ocean. Weary of its iterated falling
In the eye, he turns away. And the sound of it
Diminishes room after room. The cradle
Of its cry grows distant and dim, and then
Stops. And the gaze of it turns toward the sky.
But night and day, my heart, incessant ocean
Shakes the shore. And the shaken grave cries out
Across the fields, the flowery meadows, and the moor.

22.

Beyond the window, in the failing light,
The hot balloons are cold, the raptured neighbors
Drag along the ground. The philosopher looks back
Toward ocean: first, the flats, and then the white
Surf-line through mist, and then like night the deep
That is full of wonders and the dark where
Wanders the *Great Eastern*. And he beholds
The parrot, last speaker of the extreme
Language, who flies before: *"Awk! Follow me."*

IV.

SONG OF THE KEY

23.

Between the land and ocean is a gate
With a hard lock. There *is* a key. (Not this
Key, and not that one; but one of these. Maybe
It is, as is often thought, the key marked
"Ocean.") The turning of the key is the one
Action of a life—presented as marriage.
In any case, the bird is on the wing:
The vessel launched that under sail and steam
(Impatient engines) masters space and time.

24.

—There is a child who has a key in hand.
His mother is looking away, and his brother
Is looking away. *But he has a key.*
Shall it be that at first it does not fit?
But then at last after much fumbling, and
Striking of the plate, the key does fit;
And turns in the lock and the night opens,
And its hours are yours? The child has a key.
What does the key fit? Does it fit the night?

25.

The child has a key to the *night*. But the night
Does not have a lock that opens with a key!
How then shall he enter the night? What means
Shall he take in hand. —"He shall take in hand
The sail and the steering oar, and go forth
On the open sea. O sailor, by the ways
Of the night you will reach the distant islands
Of night, and by the means of sail and oar
Will come, after much wandering, to night's door."

26.

And the child has a key for *pain*. But pain
Does not have a lock that opens with a key.
How then shall he follow the worm in the tooth?
And how ascend the winding stair of the worm
To that high room of the wound, where the lady
Of pain still weaves her web, unto this death.
By what means, philosopher, go that way?
—"By permission of the lady who says:
'The night has come. Rise up, and follow me.'"

27.

The child has a key to the *snow*, and also
To the treasuries of the snow. But the snow
Does not open with a key. Nor do its treasuries.
For the snow comes and goes in its own time
—As you know—in the patience of the weather.
And the treasuries of the snow, the beauty
Of her astounding body (the wonder cabinet
Of his study), she may or may not show;
And only to the one who pleases her.

28.

Sailor! Does the *ocean* open with a key?
"*Oh yes*. The key with the 'ocean' mark." . . .
After the deaths at the winches and the freezing
Of the heart, our ship of prophecy—*Great
Eastern*—casting off the chains of the launching
(Like Houdini, the poetic Jew)
Goes down the estuary, with a shout
From the direction of the keeper of the pleas
(In fact, the coroner), to ocean —and is out

29.

Among the contesting elements: —the cities
Where there is no breath, and walls with a collapsing
Gate, and synagogues, mills, and shopping malls
All water—and the universities of dream
That summon the philosophical Professor
Of Felicity—that gazing man with pain
In his mouth: a tooth that hurts and must be
Taken out. (It is, as one might say, the worm
Of truth.) —He has looked a long time. And now

30.

What does the philosopher see? —The citizens
Who have ceased to believe in "reasons of state"
Forsake their schools. Some great purpose—"Justice!
For the Living and the Dead"—blazes upon
The foreheads of the passengers aboard
This ship of fools: the man from the synagogue
And the girls from the mill, the shopping mall,
The University—seduced (By whom?
The perfumed sailor of the iron ship,

31.

Great Eastern, which is the winter sun)
To voyage among the islands of ocean.
"Once aboard the lugger," the sailor mutters,
"And the girls are mine!" —What does the philosopher
See from his window? Above the bow, aflame,
Bright bird, the minister of love and fame,
Antipodean parrot who can remember
(The only one!) the language of his Lord,
The god he follows like a winged dog.

V.

ENTERTAINMENT ON DECK

32.

"Awk! This is the last judgement of the world,"
He says. "I am your maker. And *you* go
To meet your kind among the islands. And there
You will behold her face and kiss her eyes."
—Night comes on and a premonitory rain.
High up above the deck, shrouded in mists,
Subject to the winds of the universe
And to the vessel's motion, there rise and fall
The families of *aerialists* who never miss:

33.

One cries, "What is?", "What do you know?" The other
From the mast replies, "My dear, it is 'thus and so.'"
"Hold me!" "Keep me from harm!" "We are in one another's
Arms." —And thus, discoursing to and fro (The air
Resounds with what they do, and do not, know),
They throw themselves upon the heartless winds.
But I see no one fall despite the weather,
The great swell on the water, and the rising storm.

34.

And now, look down! On gorgeous wagons, lashed
Between each pair of the six masts below,
Mongolian *contortionists*—three women
Raised on mountains, as it were, above the blown
And streaming deck where lies the ship's cat drowned.
"Ladies and gentlemen! This art, elsewhere unknown,
Presents the body and the soul as they converse
In the language of their intimate captivity,
One to the other, syllable and verse.

35.

See how, untroubled by the tempest, two
Doves and another bird (significant
Of hope), all white, flutter upon the upward
Palm of one 'sky-pointing' foot.'' —By this ex-
Otic trick is shown the labyrinthine word
Or knot—the patient heart—that is perpetually
The care of three Mongolian women,
Masters of thought, who, with their birds in air,
Turn slowly like the ocean upon mountains.

36.

What is *this* art? Good Gollie, Miss Molly,
My heart. Look at *the clowns that juggle jars,*
Sometimes with the hand, sometimes with the foot.
They are sitting on the gunnels in the rain.
Each stares at his own. Each feels the heaving deck.
Each smells the dead cat (drowned), and says aloud:
"Under *these circumstances,* it's a helluva act."
The rule of juggling jars is this: At birth
They give you one. You throw it up and down

37.

To the satisfaction of everyone,
And at your death bequeath it (as they say,
"In turn") unbroken to the next one on,
Your "son." "And the jar," says the dead cat (drowned),
"It is of course your heart." —Patience! O patience
Is ever kind. And patience is not weary,
Patience is as unexhaustible as wind
Which never varies from its high concerns:
The wave, the shaken bough, the shadow in the wood.

38.

And what is, then, the poet's work! —Patience.
As when the mother says, "Do this," or "Do not";
Or the father; or the sea-wind which is always
Saying to the sailor, "Go, my man"; or "Go
About"; or the parrot, death's harbinger,
Declares: "The jar is broken like a heart
Under the weight of thought." Then, what? What
Shall the poet say to the mother or father,
The exhausted heart? What shall he do?

VI.

SONG OF THE CONSTANT NYMPH

39.

—The poet mounts the stair. He labors upward still.
"Short of breath and shorter . . . ," he climbs the tower
To the top—the *camera obscura* of our death
In air. On the cliff above the gorge the poet,
In the coldest weather, ascends—first one
Step and then another one—into the final
Chamber, at the poet's hour: What does he hear?
Whispers from the graves upon the shore? —*"The world
Is an indefinite demand beyond our power."*

40.

Heart! Only in the *camera obscura*
Of our death can we detect (so short of
Breath we are) the cry. A rising mist
Extinguishes the material eye. But from afar,
Upon the moor above, there comes the song
Flung by the Constant Nymph across the Avon,
"I have no friend. Alas! Only the salt
Sea-mill, creating and destroying, of
The world's demand is real: IF YOU LOVE ME

41.

SING ME SOMETHING." —*Who says, "I have no friend"?*
So says the tree. So says the bird. So says
The cloud. So say the moon, the moor, the flower,
And every grain of sand—each one a world.
(So Blake!) And every minute of every hour.
What is the labor, then? What is the work?
"Patience—Niobe of the hill who weeps
(The salt sea-mill), and stares at history.

42.

Therefore, let us make a stir in the shadows,
Like a gust of summer wind among the leaves
Of the garden—a sea-wind, come in its time
From ocean, that shakes the leaves and the shadows
Of the leaves, and passes back in its time
To ocean; and, as it passes, brings to mind
A fashion of the web-like dark and light.
We have more to say to one another under
The Tree of Life, among shadows in the garden: —

43.

"What have you lost?"—"O, I have lost my friend."
"How shall I know her if she walks this way?"
—"My friend is a person with a patient look."
"There are many such under the blue sky."
—"The friend whom I have lost carries a book."
"What does that book the woman carries say?"
—"It is a text of weight. The story of a boy
Imprisoned in a labyrinth." *"How so?"*
—"Because he did not tell the truth . . ."

44.

"How did you lose your friend?" —"She is the shining
Harvest of a fruitful summer, abundant
Rain, and the earth of the Great Work Farm —reaped,
Raked, shocked, stacked, threshed, and carried home in the wide
Rick and stored in barns against the worm, the want,
The winter storm. But, like a torn seed-sack
Dragged through a wilderness, the mind is thin,
Vacant, soiled, never at rest. And the grain
Is lost, like truth. And the friend is gone."

''*What is her name?*'' —''She is the Constant Nymph
Who keeps a windy house upon the moor,
Sea-facing, far away, and stares (as I have said)
At history.'' ''*And if we meet, what will she say?*''
—''Her word will be: 'Poet, I have come down
Among the shadows to lead you out of darkness
Into day. The darkness opens with *this* key.'''
''*And what shall I reply?*'' —''If you should see
Her with her weighty book, upon the roads,

Say this: 'Living or dead, the boy has spread
His wings and gone among the birds, the last
Speaker of the extreme language—poetry.
And the bird has gone to sea, as supercargo,
The Parrot of the Ship, *Great Eastern*, launched
In the darkest hour before dawn, side-
Wise, into Thames, to the applause of the Mayor,
The coroner (the keeper of the pleas), etc.,
On her maiden voyage, southward, through the storm!'''

VII.

THE PARROT'S STORY

47.

"How did it feel, when you became a bird?"
—"I changed my sex, which was before a boy's.
At the darkest hour before dawn I learned
The other part of the song—the thorough-bass
Of the wind in shadows, and the spectral anthem
Of the mind in grass. When the scattered elements
Assembled, the form was strictly speaking *not*
Your kind. I had become, of better things,
A sulphur-headed parrot. *This boy had wings.*"

48.

"How did it *feel?*" —"Well, it was not like age
(Age takes the human form); nor yet like growing
Wise or beautiful, nor 'having a good
Time.' Nor was it an atrocious pain, *pace*
The torturers of the king (from the Ukraine).
I wept because I had become an Anti-
Podean with a prophecy—but (awk!) to whom?—
Uttering words nobody knows. *Such* is the sorrow
Of the boy who has gone among the birds.

49.

But to fly is another matter. My Heart!
Flight is the world's work which is to rise
Uttering loud cries in the extreme languages
Of storm (tears blinding my still human eyes)
And meet by patient stroking of the oars
The children of the night in air: Aëllo
(Her face is beautiful. Her hair is gray.)
And her sisters born from the barren sea
Who take my sex. And whisper, 'Ecstasy!'

50.

She was inseminated by winter rain
Upon the aged body that sleeps alone,
Ocean—("Who is this pilgrim on my belly?"
"What is this burden on my bone?")—and born
Wrapped in her own hair, and laid in the cradle
Of the hurricane. Follow now Aëllo,
Cyclonic dream of ignorance and passion.
Climb the pilgrim stairway of her womb,
And hear the shifting of the midnight stone

51.

Which is the sun—as it is making ready
In the darkest hour before the dawn
To rise in splendor above Jerusalem."
—May we hear it once again, you and I,
Who are brothers and sisters on that ocean,
Birds of the storm (wrapped in Aëllo's hair),
Pilgrims on her womb—("How changed from what we were!")—
At the end of time, in the hour of the wreck,
In the hour of the dark myth of the heart.

52.

A thunderous turning of the lock . . . !
—"Behold! The Gate of Night," exclaims the parrot.
"Awk!" She strikes the metal with her beak.
"Tell me! Does the darkness open with a key?"
And the keepers of the Gate reply, "O yes!
(This parrot speaks Antipodean: —the extreme
Language of the poet.) *The bird must pass
Out of the night.*" Thus, the keepers of the Gate,
The Water Spout and plated Behemot.

VIII.

THE GATE OF NIGHT

53.

—Philosopher! Above the gorge of Avon,
At the high window of your observation,
Your silent *camera* amid the snows,
Narrowing your vision now at evening
(The darkness falls on ocean), read the lesson
Written, on the midnight Gate which is the end
Of thought (the sailor's perpetual delight
In motion), by the Master, glorious but fatal,
Of the *Great Eastern*: Isambard Brunel.

54.

For it is common to follow the sun,
Or that we make the sun itself our vessel
Of the western trade. From the first morning
Arousal, always late, when the low light
Burns through the closed lids and the eyes open
At last, and a pillar of light is seen
In motion on the wall (and all the while
A woman has been pretending to read
A book, since the beginning of the world).

55.

It is common (I say) to follow the winter
Sun all day to the south and west, throw out
The sail of the mind to the ocean road
When the wind is free. Or the impatient engine
Of the heart takes up the work. All courses
Lead to the "dark harbor," the end of thought,
At the horizon where the iron Gate
Of Night erects itself, and the sea-road stops.
And from the wreck there rises the sailor's song:

56.

"Brunel, Brunel, builder of the ship to Hell,
What have you written on the iron gate,
Socketed in stone, that opens with a key
(The sex of a boy!)—guarded by the Behemot
With plates and Water Spout that monstrous worm
Beneath whose million feet are strewn the wrecks
That fill the *wunderkammer* of the storm?
O God, God, God! God! Can *this* be your secret,
These explosions, this wasting, and this burning?"

57.

What does the poet know, mutest of men,
Whose language is the extreme silence of
The Antipodes, the other islands of the world,
And whose countenance human or inhuman
As the case may be, a face that is always
Forming, ineffaceable, as the shore
Comes and goes and is always shaping
And reshaping the ocean under wind,
Earliest of us, before all things?

58.

In the beginning the poet was awake—
When the heaven and earth were not yet formed,
The wilderness of storm unplanted
And the fields of the farm. Then the god did it
With outstretched arm. By a strange blow built
The Gate of Night and turned away from the work.
But the poet saw it, waking with the birds,
The secret of the gods. And did turn back
Through music to the other side of the dark.

59.

—Laughing and weeping we set sail on ocean;
And came at sundown, by means of the steering oar,
To the Gate of Night, nearby the Cave of Voices
Where Vedic frogs adorn themselves with song.
One frog cries out: "My Lord! You are my father
And my son!" And another frog replies, "My sister!
My only one!" In Chorus, then, beside
The solemn water, all the frogs: "The Lord
Reveals a word, the body of his bride."

60.

And on the Gate of Night, far out in ocean
(Night of the marriage, gate of the marriage night),
Behold designed, the picture of the sulfur-
Headed, loud, poetic bird—that was a boy—
Who is now fire. *You* heard the prophecy:
"He shall take in hand the sail and the steering oar
And come, after much wandering, to night's door."
"The night" (so sing the frogs) *"does* open with a key.
Give us a kiss!" (That's what *frogs* always say.)

IX.

SONG OF THE KISS

61.

—But who is that, weeping, so close to myself?
Who if not the wind? What do I hear? What?
The sorrows of the Fate, the Constant Nymph
Who stares at history, the flaming bride.
In fact the wind does rise about the gate;
Extraordinary tides announce the storm.
Far off, it is the merest trace of thought.
But, then, like logic, or a freight train underground,
Inexorable—close to the ear—profound:

62.

The voice of the storm. My heart! What *do*
I hear? What? *"The destiny of desire*
Whom we call our Lord is the history
Of the world." Cities are in the picture: Rome,
Jerusalem, Dundee, and Baltimore;
Also Aëllo whose hair is grey; and ocean
Heaving up great weight of water. The elephants
Are calm. The aerialists, despite the storm,
Sing psalms. The drowned cat affirms his glory.

63.

"No other Master than this bird!" it cries.
—The marriage is consummated. In water,
Fire burns. (This is not miracle, but love!)
What do you hear, Professor of Felicity?
What rock and roll out of that cave? Here come
The voices, exalted and thrown down in tears,
From the Cave of Voices, making the sea salt:
"Sailors are neither living nor dead. Ships
Never rest. Launched—thereafter, they are never still."

64.

And the marriage kiss, O my beloved,
Is of the face—the face that is never
At rest, neither living nor dead: a sailing
Banner, a wanderer island after island,
Subject to the lightning and the hurricane
On the salt-road and great wave, and the shock
Of the white squall, unsurvivable, until
At last, "Landfall to windward!" Then, the beat
Against weather to anchorage and make fast

65.

At the far shore. And we shelter in this rock.
Look! —The stone limbs of a great loom are here,
That weave the web of wonder, an imperial
Tent of two entrances: "To Go" and "To Come"—
A large room. And here are wells of water
From far away, and the resounding hives
Of the honey bee, and mixing bowls for the wine
Of earth and heaven. Drag hither, O my heart,
Your treasure tied with a Circean knot.

66.

—Thus, in the Spring of the year, after Autumn
Storms and Winter rains, the leaves of the year
In their multitudes lie lovely and low
On the forest floor, down-fallen (as we do)
To death. The man and woman, then, walk out
Along the ocean-shore as far as the monument.
They sing to one another: —"Felicity is this kiss."
"This kiss is thee." There stands the water-oak,
Tree of two seasons, in the patience of the tree.

67.

And there Justice is born, child of the kiss,
Between the land and water where everything
Speaks and is silent. The reed speaks to the wave
And bends to hear the reply of the wave.
And both look up to the wind, for the wind
Has much to do: —Mornings, bearing seed out
On ocean where it cannot grow. —Evenings,
Bringing ashore the songs of the mariners
From ocean that sleeps, as it seems, or not.

X.

THE SHIPWRECK

68.

But, in fact, the death-ship (of Isambard
Brunel) has run against the Gate of Night—
Destiny of thought. And the philosophical
Professor of Felicity, without his wife,
Has suddenly arrived, by reason of a wreck,
Together with the parrot (a winged boy
Who should have known), hard by the Tree of Life.
The great saloon, adorned with mirrors (Second
Deck), explodes, and all the dancers die!

69.

—Have I come too late, then, to my own mind,
Having come at midnight to the blind gate
Where thought is blocked, and feints, ends, or turns back?
Or, strange to contemplate, starts out another
Way, unthought, not to be thought or thought of,
Up-wind, faking, in the dark, on the stark
Hill of the sea-road? And the dawn surprised
When the wind shifted, the ship fell off,
And I lost the landfall in the waking,

70.

Myself, hungry to see, not able to see,
Not seeing (who cannot answer so intense
A glance) the near-at-hand, most hidden. And all
The while the sound of waves breaking somewhere
On an unseen shore. So now, chronometer in hand,
I tell by time the space of the sea room
(How far? How long?) which is the unmade bed
Of ocean, restless body that sleeps alone.
How wrong the time is, unconsolable

71.

And red! For the *Great Eastern* is wrecked
On a rock in Dundrum Bay, the County Down,
Under the Mountains of Mourne. And the gigantic
Hulk of iron plates is thinning out, while
Southward storm clouds, sinister vaticans
Of thought, unleash their shadows which pursue
Like dogs the inconsolable heart they haunt
And kill. Who will sing the requiem? The frogs
And the Ukrainian torturers of the king.

72.

—*This wreck is the beginning of the work.*
"Short of breath," the last master of truth,
The poet, ascends the stair—up to the *camera
Obscura* of our death in air—(Have you forgot?)—
And takes a look! He sees the monument;
The motion of the sea; the wreck of thought;
The aimless Professor of Felicity; and (far off!)
The Tree. The poet affronts the Gate of Night,
Loud bird at hand, breathless, blind and late:

73.

Solus sapiens, hic homo. The only
Wakeful mind among the dead. *He has looked
Back.* Standing at the rail for hours, in all
Kinds of weather, he stares at the wake of
The wide ship. As one might listen to the song
(Not heard now, but seen as in a mirror
Large as ocean) of the sailor who has
Turned around and come ashore. *Follow that one*
And enter in the other side of the story.

XI.

THE PATIENCE OF TREES

74.

"—Does the Gate of Night turn *outward*, when it
Opens, upon a rank, familiar courtyard
Where is a dung-heap and the village well,
To which the sailor (followed by the swineherd,
A serious man, self-taught) comes home (all
Ignorance and passion spent) and seats himself
In the sun against the palace wall, and there
Considers sleep? . . . At noon, the sailor says
To the serious man: 'Everything moves!'

75.

Or does the Gate of Night turn *inward* on
The wonder closet of the heart, where lie
The secrets, each at rest, with folded wings
And crossed feet like winds fallen or histories
Of peace, dreaming of Justice (child of the kiss),
The perpetual study of Felicity?
—*The Gate of Night turns inward*. Images cease:
'Shadows in the path,' says the serious man,
'Of the *Great Eastern*—which is the Winter sun.'"

76.

Where is the landfall at the end of thought,
The reddest beaches? How will the children know,
Who follow after us, *where we were wrecked*
And on what rock we split, and for what reasons?
Say, "*The Tree of the Two Seasons* is the mark
Planted in time, fragrant in the noon's heat,
To blossom in eternity a light. And the sailor,
Black with salt and naked as a foot, waits out
The weather, like a spark in a pail, at its root."

Among living things, the patient ones are trees.
And among trees, the oak at the shore is master
Of patience. —When the thought of this and that
Founders, and all the sailors on ocean cry:
"Where are we? *This storm is irresistible!*",
And when the wind blows from desolate and unpeopled
Crossings of the working water, far out
Where there is no watchman and there is no gaze:
Then, the trees bend—a grace—nothing—and enough.

. . . Sound, now, of the wind in the Tree of Life
At the shore. —But anyone who looks does not
See. Or another who listens does not hear.
Speech reveals itself as a loving wife
Intricately dressed reveals her body—
Never mind how. Or as the voices of friends
Will keep the treasures of the wandering sailor
Secure with knots of mysterious blessings
And cover him over with leaves of two seasons.

Not dead—yet—or dying—(not at this moment)—
But the sea's cry in his ear, and the whole
Body stretched still on the long meter of water,
From which the world wears—and the hills arise
Again as in the beginning, and fall down
As at the end they will. In the sleep of the sailor,
Weary of her insomniac obsession,
Ocean whispers, "Do not be afraid of repetition
—A song in which the images have ceased."

80.

The patient life. What is it? —The patient woman
And the patient man each morning *turn,* together
With the other patient ones: the living, the dead,
And the unborn. They turn and look one way,
At the earth and sky. "It will be fine," they say.
Or, "It will be trouble. The wind is in the tree."
Each washes the body that is her own,
Looks seaward, and listens to the sailors' song
As they walk the ruddy beaches, up and down:—

81.

"The wind is in the tree at the end of thought
Where the ploughman sleeps at noon in the root
And the iron plough delays—until the ploughman
Wakes cursing his lot, and then turns back
Toward the row just opened in the field
And the sod to break. Swimmer! How does it feel
To endure *the demand of being at all*
By a patient renewal of the stroke:
This great work, the iron plough, the gaudy wreck."

82.

And what have you lost, man of the sea-roads?
The winds rise. The trees speak in many voices.
"I have come to the beaches of the South
Hard by the Gate of Night. And in my mouth
A rotten tooth . . ." —Then, slowly, the Tree of Life
Inverts itself, like a Mongolian acrobat.
And its leaves come down among us, laughing
And shaking bright hands like prayers. And the white
Dove of the answering glance inflates her throat . . .

XII.

THE INVISIBLE CIRCUS

83.

In the room a woman pretends to read
A book. The lamp beside her chair still burns,
Although it is long since day. And the boy
With a key—or perhaps a paper—is gone.
The pillar of light which rested on the floor
Behind him, and leaned against the wall,
Is flickering out. At evening the woman says,
"There is work to be done. I am alone.
Everything moves, and the night comes on."

84.

—"These are the Antipodes, home of birds,"
Says the parrot. And then, in a loud voice,
"The soul is *not* alone!" —The parrot, sulphur-headed
Like a flame, and the poet "short of breath,"
Stand up *and look one way*. Behind them, the Gate
Of Midnight and the monsters of the deep
Of thought, which are the Water Spout and plated
Behemot. Before them the patient Tree
In its two seasons (time and eternity)

85.

And, beyond that, the landscape of the kiss
Of which the child dreams at the breast. "This bird
Is *Antipodean*," says the poet, "a human spirit
Looking for its gardens. He is the last
Speaker of the extreme language—sovereign
Tool of the Great Work. Let him increase!
For I am short of breath and must grow less,
Cool, and disperse like ash." And so the parrot
Enters history, through the Gate of Night,

As fire and light, Master of the Work,
Sweet whistler of desire in the dark.
And flames on the monument, the shadowy room
In which the Constant Nymph as in a Labyrinth,
Sits all day alone, she of the white demand:
"On pain of death (or life), YOU SING ME SOMETHING."
The aerialists who swam ashore with ease
Have re-erected their trapeze. As soon
As they have dried their hair, you'll hear them in

The air resume their anthem as before:
—"Now I am wise." —"My dear, it must be so.
I see your eyes; and they are full of tears."
—"What of the years?" —"Look there!" —"Where?" —"There! Below."
Like a gigantic animal on an iron
Stool the *universe* goes round—to the diminishing
Applause of men from the synagogue, girls
From the mill (the mall, the university),
And the ship's cat drowned. Then, they disappear.

The "entertainment" on the shore *is now*
Invisible. But at the darkest hour,
The hour before the dawn, a spectral circus
Can be seen suspended in an angle of
The moon (a labyrinth, or shadowy room)—
No breath, no light, no sound. The Greatest Show
On Earth. There the Mongolian contortionists
Still turn on mountains. But their birds are gone.
And the juggler is combing the hair of his son.

89.

In the room a woman rises and stares
At the evening sky. Night is coming on,
Winter, and the hurricane. "Where is the light,"
She asks, "when it is not with me? Where can it
Be found? Has it fallen down like the leaf
And the rain, and does it lie then in the ground
Among the other things without a history?
Where is the child who is gone from this room?
Maybe in the ground, like the winter sun?"

XIII.

WHAT WHITE BIRD

90.

—(What beats against the window of the philosopher
And his bride? What white bird—body of death—
Wild with its own concern—breaks casement and pane,
The night coming on, winter, and the hurricane?
She covers her shoulders and head with a shawl.
But the bird of storm has entered the room
(The terror is in her hair!), and beats against
The wall, and strews the floor with torn white wings
And heaps up the lost limbs of the first snow.

91.

By what means, philosopher, rid the room
Of the wild white dove that fouls the floor?
—"Oh! Do it with a broomstick or a broom!",
Says the astonished bride. "In any case,
Your strong right arm." *But the bird of death
Has blundered in.* How drive it out again
Among the rocks, the bloody sands, the pelicans?
"Sing against it," says the Tree of Life
To the Professor of Felicity.

92.

"Sing against it!" "In the name of the rock,
The root, the lock, the key." The Tree bends down
Beneath the weight of storm and chants the bourdon.
"Drive the worm from the tooth, pain from the mouth.
And from the cloth, the rust and moth. And the snow
From the hearth." —But the dove of death has entered
The room, not to be driven out again.
The snow across the threshold rustles in the wind:
"Allen!" (it knows my name!) "I am the white demand.")—

XIV.

THE WORK

93.

The window of the philosopher is broken.
The storm is *in the room*. The night comes on
And the bird of destruction. Out of the gorge
Of Avon shout the Vedic frogs: "Clear the mouth."
"Draw the tooth." "Heal the breath." "Mount to the tower
Of your observation, *camera obscura*
Of our death (or life), and speak the truth:
'The poem is the poet's labyrinth!'"

94.

And so we come, in age, after a hundred
Thousand turnings (versing blackens the page),
To hear far off the earliest cry
Of the garden bird—the nightingale—
In the darkest hour, the hour before dawn,
When the wind is fallen down. "Philosopher,"
Says the bird. "The soul is not alone. Now come!
(A steady finger on the left-hand wall)
Into the garden—through the gate of horn."

95.

—Not sailors now, nor swimmers, nor men of the oar,
We do not speak in figures, we do not
Speak . . . This is the landscape of the heart
Where is the gazing-ball in which the sun
Moves not, nor in its turn the silver moon.
Here is a water-oak, the Tree of Life
In its mysterious well, and paths of stone
Among the shrubs and trees. How quiet it is!
Listen now! to the birds and the bird-songs:

XV.

SONG OF THE BREAKING OF CLOCKS AND SCALES

96.

"By scales we are weighed, by clocks our time
Is told. But by what justice, by what steady
Hand, *by what reliable decree?* —The lust
Of the boy is pure. His rage against
The mystery of clocks and scales is just.
The steel of the case he cracks on the rocks,
The glass of the scales he breaks. And the gears
Of clocks and scales, that signify desire,
Poured out on stone, are perfect—every one.

97.

He does not open the clock-case with a key,
Nor the glass of the scales. Not with the key
Of night, and not with the key of pain, and not
With the key of ocean. *He breaks the box on stone.*
He knows the secret is within, the solitary one:
The justice of the perfect wheel—the dead,
The living, the unborn—is the desire of the boy.
But now (alas!) destruction is in the room
(A reliable decree) and the snow comes down."

98.

The evening clocks and the morning clocks
Pass from heaven to heaven. The poet is in tears.
She is in tears. But the birds sing on
Under the winter sun. "We are the lovers
Who make one another wise. And the wisdom
That we give and take is like a kiss.
When we die, it does not die. But it goes up
Among the heavens of light. When the sun shines,
It is the shadow of sun in the garden."

99.

At the edge of the garden, near the flowery
Hedge, the garden borders on the meadow.
The meadow path flows down—and pours the gathered
Flowers of all our wandering into the ocean.
At the shore is a grave, the labyrinth
Of a long life. There, hand in hand, we walk
To the human end. —Between the garden and
The meadow, in the lofty hedge, there dwell
The big winds of the universe like souls.

100.

"What have you lost?" The big winds call to me,
Which are never still. And the Tree of Life
Bends down, in the patience of the tree. The leaves
Of the tree are yellow: some are on the ground
Below, some on the shaken bough in the great
Streams of the soul. And nothing else is true:
"The big winds try the patience of the Tree.
Death is in the garden—a reliable decree!
The soul is not alone, because of you . . ."

XVI.

THE DELAY OF THE ANSWERING GLANCE

101.

When does the year begin, philosopher?
At the rains? After the drought of summer,
When the seed has taken its death to heart
And forgotten its destiny? —Or at the snows?
When the garden itself forgets its avenues
And quiet walks, for one or two; and the gazing-
Ball looks and looks, and sees nothing at all?
Does the year begin at the snows? At the snows,
Philosopher? . . . When *does* the year begin?

102.

Is it upon the midnight of the frozen
Lake, after a long, silent winter day,
When dawn is announced at the black heart
Of the ice by thunderous explosions
In its chains, for an invisible sun
Has touched the lake, unseen at midnight by
The skaters who labor among the islands
Of winter on the darkest road—with patient
Renewals of the stroke—and fear the sound

103.

Which prophesies the cold release of water
Into water? —How, then, will we get home
Before the flood of dawn and the end of time?
How will the man on the dark road who is stirred
At heart return? —*When does the year begin?*
Is it punctual, in the spring of the seasons,
Between the cry of the nightingale and the arrow
Of the lark or sparrow, at the moment of
Breath intaken, between the light and the sorrow?

104.

In time, there comes a time, philosopher,
When the thinking stops, and the ocean sleeps
On its hard bed and the seafarer on ocean's
Bosom sleeps—when the use of the oar is lost
And there is no more seafaring. In time,
There comes a time, philosopher, the time
Between the calling out of thought—the calling out
And the crying for it—and then, after a while,
The telling of the history of the heart

105.

In the delay of the answering glance.
In that time the great world rises up
After a long night of snow. And on high
The heaven and earth are finished and the poem
Of it. —The woman is looking away.
She is reading the book of the Winter sun.
Her lamp burns on and on into the day.
But everything remains to be done. —Therefore,
We work and wait, and submit to one another

106.

In silence. The world grows up, an oak-tree,
Slow growing and slow also to decay, planted
By the gods long dwindling out, like dowagers,
By measureless delay (in which the islands
Of romance rise from their sea) the patience
Of the heart that has no destiny
Except the answering glance. And desire
Builds the cities of ocean, with infinite
Avenues like an obsessive rhyme. And thus defers
The end of the poem and the beginning of time.

107.

At the autumn of the year, the woman
Rises, adjusts her dress, and then looks out.
She looks around at the work of the gods.
"The world is made," she says. "It is finished!
And the white dove of the answering glance
Stirs in the forest of green shrubs and trees
And the dark pools. She inflates her throat to
Utter answers. She will delay no longer
(Although the lamp still burns) to make an end:

XVII.

WEEPING BIRDS

108.

"'To be in any form. . . . what is it?'
Are the verses of the dove. 'Death' is the bourdon."
—She is like a man or a woman satisfied
By a caress or a day's work, and awake
In the darkest hours before the dawn,
The hours of greatest simplicity,
Her strenuous lover finally asleep,
Happy for a while to be alone,
Happy to weep at dawn when the birds weep,

109.

Each bird for the lover of her heart,
First one bird and another one. And, then,
The answering glance and the white dove's song!
—So, too, the boy (hero of this romance)
Comes to the end of the knowledge of the birds
(Each kind has its knowledge—*and its death*).
"My heart!" cries the boy who has found his words:
"I am a slave in another Country where
The soul is alone and out of breath."

110.

Thereafter, the weeping birds reveal themselves
By anthems in the garden. They sing for him
Invisibly all day among the shrubs, green plants
And trees. And they do not sleep at night
But lie awake, like a girl in a strange bed,
Waiting for the time to begin her weeping
When light rises bringing to the body
Knowledge of its death. —But now the white
Dove has gathered in the boy and the boy's breath:

111.

"You cannot hear a cry, and you know nothing;
Or you hear a cry and then hear another
And at the moment before death you hear
Them all—weeping—and your ignorance
Is profound, because in truth we have seen
And heard nothing and we say, 'Not all of death,
Not death (the grave, perhaps, but not itself,
But not the death) is opened with a key.'
Not this one nor that one, not any."

112.

—What, then, is the figure of experience?
The poet is dead. The extreme language has
No rememberer, no book that can be opened
To the very page and read, no passing face
That can be greeted by a public word,
No secret song. Therefore, we must take care
We are not stopped by a loud hail from high
Above us on the pilgrim way, that cannot
Be passed by, or from the Cave of Voices: "Yo!"

113.

"Yo!" Out of Machpelah leaps the Atlantic
Cable through the Gates of Night from the holy
Shore where the Gates have been open a long time.
And down the pilgrim way there comes a broken
Choir ("The Lord is One"), gathered by the bell,
Trying to say how it feels to be murdered
While praying. —And what *was* on their minds
When their prayer went up, faltered halfway,
Fell back to the human world, and stopped?

114.

What did father Abraham say to his wife,
Sarah, and what did she reply, those weeping birds
A long time in the dark? —Awake in the hour
Of greatest simplicity, the father sees the world
And the world comes to the mind of the father.
The Constant Nymph reads on—("My childen are
Killing my children," she sighs)—and her word
Passes through the body of everything
That speaks. On the pilgrim way is heard

115.

The extreme language of love. The boy changes
His form and of the previous form is not
A wrack. The parrot (Awk!) is gone. The boy
Is free to flow as water flows in water,
As grasses burn in fire, or as the earth
In winter, patient Mother, serving at last
Herself alone, passes toward the cold contentment
Of the stone. —I who was young am now old
Bent over my text (it must be this one),

116.

Baffled, and in despair and yet intent
In any case upon my truth. I will be-
Come bone of the spring earth. Not that I do
Not also become a serpent and its slough,
Or the singing bead in the web and the ex-
Piration of that bead in the bright
Air, or a beautiful man or woman
And the death (*Boha*) of each—separate
And yet the death. *But it is that the last*

117.

Form that follows the last breath, by reason
Of its freedom, is not the truth. —The weeping
Birds are calling to one another in the garden:
"There are no shining circles, joyous returns!
We go from one to another state of being,
As day is followed by the night, and night
By day is followed island after island.
Everything changes!" —The weeping birds are
Calling, and the world is coming to be.

XVIII.

THE SONG OF THE SWINEHERD

118.

"There has to be a man or woman in the world
Who is as old as the world," says the serious
Man, prophetic swineherd. Perhaps a Jew!
—"*Thus I follow her* whom I remember, and also
Do not remember, and of the remembered
And unremembered following the unremembered
One to serve her vanity and her desire
Who has been on the road with book and servant-
Animals since the beginning of the world,

119.

Before the clocks and scales began to pass
From heaven to heaven of the moon and sun
And the pillar of light moved on the wall . . . .
—*Or follow him,* whom I remember
And do not remember who is asleep
In the root like a foot, and talking to him,
The sailor wrecked upon our shore together
With his parrot, his prophecy, and his treasure,
Who has come and is yet to come. And being

120.

As I am a serious man, and patient,
Above all a follower, a man of the hog,
The dog, the labyrinth of earth, the nymph,
And the weather—I know that everything
Speaks—the living speak and the dead speak
('Justice!' they cry). And that the clocks and scales
That pass from heaven to heaven keep the time
Until the sailor comes ashore—or the god
Throws down his lightning to make an end.

121.

In the farm at the shore the voices of men
And women at the last moment before death,
Or punctually at the moment *after* the last
Breath, congregate among prophetic animals
(The hog, the crow, the dog) putting their questions.
Their voices echo in the labyrinth.
'Which road?' they ask. The animals reply,
'You must take the road assigned.' They bark and caw,
'Walk *that* way.' All point. *'And sleep on straw.'* ''

122.

Swineherd! What, then, is the *difference* of life?
''In life you can lie down in any dark.
But it is better if the bed be high
And clean, and better if there is a window
In the eastern wall. We sleep where we can
(Says he) with eyes open, listening to the birds.
But to awake entirely requires a bed-
Place, and a winter dawn, the patience to lie
Alone, and the luck of the sailor's song.''

XIX.

NO SHIP RETURNS

123.

The gaudy sailor, in full song, unknots
The Circean knots of his golden treasure,
As the lady taught him (—"knot and unknot"—)
Through whose body he sailed erect to the underworld
Of shadow, and back again full of weariness
And weeping—for she taught him, as I say,
To knot *and to unknot* the cords, in whose arms
He rested who never rests. And much is given
And nothing can be lost, because of the lady.

124.

The sailor has arisen from his sleep
In the root where he lay down at night
Like a naked foot. And on the ruddy beaches,
Among the stones, he now unwraps his fetchings
From the other islands and lays them
Beside the monument in the winter sun:
Testaments inscribed on silk; and porcelain
Depictions of the storm; gems of the darkest mine;
Grief-stones of the ocean from the black shore;

125.

Nameless gifts for somebody else's wife
(The sailor is handsome enough to die for);
And coin of which the value is unknown
(For which nothing is dear enough in history).
The sailor spreads them under the patient Tree
Of Life where by the meadow-path flow down
The meadow-flowers to the shore of ocean.
Winds wander there, pilgrims of the storm,
Up and down the beaches among the strewn

126.

Vestiges of the wreck. And the winter tide
Lifts up the trailing weed, with all its animals,
And lets it fall—slowly—hunting traces
Of the last agony of the drowned dancers
(Perhaps a startled voice, among the bones,
Or somewhere a stone of witness among stones),
When the great saloon exploded (Second Deck)
And mirrors became swords and music fire:—
But the treasure of the sailor stops desire.

127.

Therefore, visible or invisible, the creatures
Come *to hear him sing.* The king, in tears
And old, remembers the launching into Thames.
The coroner (in fact, the keeper of the pleas)
In rapture notes the weather's clemencies.
The mayor of Bristol, otherwise detained
At the cold christening of the *Great Eastern,*
Shows up on time. The torturers of the king
From the Ukraine declaim: "How beautiful!

128.

O knights and ladies, the sailor's songs re-
Fresh our spirits and help us in our work."
The Mongolian contortionists, now visible,
Have put on flesh, are married, and take walks
By the seaside. "This sailor," say the girls,
"Is the best damned news since the poet died."
The Vedic frogs are practicing a vow.
And the dead cat, with lustrous eye, delights
Her lord who sings to her as to a bride,

129.

The audience of all song. And from the labyrinth
The Constant Nymph is drawn. The neighbors rise
In their balloons among the bells at evening
For it is Sunday. The scholar from the school,
The ladies from the mall, and from their gardens
Weeping birds come forth to hear the sailor's song.
He has SOMETHING TO SING and sings in tune:
"No ship returns, as the wave returns—
Or the sun in its seasons, or the moon."

130.

—But shall we say, my heart, "No ship returns,
As the wave returns"? Or shall we say, "One
Ship does not return, whether in winter
Or another season." Everything moves
But the ship is still. The sun is going down
Under Avon, and the winter night comes on.
"One ship does not return." Abandoned in a low
Lagoon and subject to the rot, the metal
Plates are thinning out, the coral worm at home.

131.

The sailor knots his treasure up again
With the hard knots taught him by the lady
To open and to close the body of love.
He rises from his throne of song. Followed by
The swineherd, the sailor walks inland. They set
Up a trophy. Then disappear—like stones
On stony ground which first you see, they are
So precious to you, but then you do not
See because there are so many the same.

XX.

A SHORT WALK TO THE HUMAN END

132.

The philosopher rises from his window.
He was staring at the ocean on its bed
Of stones, its turning, its falling in the eye
All night—as one might watch a sleepless soul
Forever passing away, and hear its cry
At the moment of passing. The philosopher
Turns at dawn from his window into the room
And walks through it into another room
And then another one, as into deeper snow.

133.

Far from the seaward window, we cannot hear
The ocean. The sound diminishes room
After room, and then stops. But the ocean will
Continue on its bed of stone . . . .
—To return to this room I have been gone
A long time, and now I must set out again
This time on foot by the only road, the flowery
One. But I also have never departed
And have been lying all this time asleep

134.

With eyes wide open in the inmost chamber
On an unmade bed. On the bed is a sheet
With a brown stain—signifying a thousand
Secrets of the body *and the soul*. At evening
We lie down to sleep on the soiled bed,
Having never departed from it and listen
To the sounds of ocean not to be outlived,
Or to the silence where that sound must be
In the place where the path comes to an end.

135.

And we depart again, by the only road
From the seashore—the meadow way and the great
Hedge of souls—inland into deeper and deeper
Snow, souls calling to souls how heaven and earth
Are never finished, the body never formed
But always changing form. —"And how shall I
Know you if you walk this way?" —"O Miss Molly,
You are sunlight on moving water, or through
The autumn forests the sound of the wind."

136.

The setting of the winter sun diffuses
Its comely lights, like the testament of
A benevolent man who has patiently chosen
This gift for *that* one, and for us this cold
Daylight: relentless, clear, and passing to
The dark, which gives no reasons and is just.
A good day for a walk at the seashore
As far as the monument. —*When the soul
Departs the body it cannot hear nor see.*

XXI.

THE IVORY HUNTERS

137.

Therefore, think *now* what you must do then—
Before the moment of death. At the moment
Of death, there is no time, or it is the wrong
Time. The dying are entirely preoccupied.
They have too much to do at the moment of
Death or they are understandably absent-minded
For they have entered on the empty world,
And left behind a dark myth still echoing
With their voices. Like the book forgotten

138.

On the pavement the summer rains erase,
All the pages of it, and that *very page*
(To be written again in a long life)
They entered at their birth in the beginning.
Hearing then the still echoing voices of
The men and women who had gone before,
Who had heard at *their* birth the still echoing
Voices of those who had gone before them,
And before them—as far as the giant ones

139.

And the stream of ocean. *As far as the gods!*
Who bequeathed to us the dark myth still echoing
With their mingled voices like the sounds of ocean
In a room where men and women once lived,
Left empty now except for the sounds of ocean
And certain shadows of all they were:
Wondrous animals, and dark men dancing
To the moon who now no longer sow and reap
But hunt the ivory for forgotten reasons

140.

In an empty world. There the people dwell
Whose destination is unfixed. They move
Mostly at night, setting out at sundown,
Restless transhumance, able to survive
Combat with the lion—huge men, and the women
That bore them—not men of the flail and sieve,
Not for a long time, or men of the oar.
But people of the elder god, among the birds
Whose mingled voices echo through the forest

141.

Like shaken bells discoursing in the dark
Of some large purpose which they understand.
My dear, you must remember at the moment
Of your death that in the world to which
You go there is a tribe who have not heard
The ocean, whose singers on the singing rocks
Enthroned amidst the freshest streams compose
At night the poems of an elder god.
—By day they hunt the elephant for ivory.

142.

Whether the royal torturers take you down,
Or whether in the paradise of time
You starve to death for want of history,
When you come to the other side of the Gate
With your key in hand and at last *A SONG*,
Master of the labyrinth, drunk with the applause
Of the Constant Nymph, then the dark myth is
Empty of you once again *and your soul*
Must be alone. —At once the cries begin

143.

In the extreme language of the poet's god,
Remembered only by a certain parrot of
The garden (*Awk!*) and poet of the patient
Stroke:—the ding and ding and dong and dong
Of waters, tones of the falls on the forest
Floor and around the stone of song on which
The singer sits among her words, in the fresh
Streams of the universe, her skirts darkened by
The vocal waters to which she tunes her throat.

XXII.

THE SOVEREIGN

144.

If you and I intend to think (as we do),
Philosopher, intend to go (*and go,*
As we have done!) the long way around, hearing
Much and seeing what there is to see
By boat—to come where we began, turning
The key twice—once to open and again,
The second time, to close and lock forever
The gates of night, then we must tell the story
Of the storm and shipwreck until the end

145.

Has come to mind, and beyond that the mind
Has come to mind—and the judgement upon mind.
For all that *was* expectation is, now, memory,
And memory is memory only at the end
When the exhausted reader turns the last page
At the extreme edge of the pilgrim way.
Behind is the whole story of the world
And before is nothing, and the man is like
A weary sailor somehow escaped the wreck

146.

("No ship returns") and rocks (the thought), who now
Looks back and dedicates a picture and also treasure
(Mostly gifts from women) tied with Circean
Knots, and vows to hang his dripping garments
Up, a trophy to the god of ocean, being
Empty both of pain and breath. Far away,
The ship goes down and rusts on the bottom
Of a lagoon. The weeping birds sing on
At set of sun across the darkening water.

147.

It is all one day. The hour before dawn
To the hour after dark—when we have read
The story to the end, and closed the book.
The sky darkens over Jerusalem.
The thunder cracks. The ship has risen from
Its wreck in sand never to rest again,
Never to return, or rest, on sea or land.
The philosopher, at the window of his death
In air, sees linked analogies without end:

148.

Brunel's responsibility for construction
Of the vast infrastructure of Great Britain
Prevented him from playing with his children.
But, on 3 April, Isambard performed his one
Conjuring trick—which consisted of putting
A gold sovereign in his mouth and taking
It out his ear. The gold coin, inadvertantly,
Slipped down his throat. He missed the opening
Of the Bristol railway as a result.

149.

On 13 May, Isambard was strapped to a hinged
Table-top and raised vertically, head
Downwards. His back was struck gently and, after
Some ordinary coughing, the coin fell out.
"It's out. It's out." The news was carried by word
Of mouth across London, and by wire to all
The nations of the empire. On that day men
Who had never sung did *sing—melodiously—*
And the applause re-echoed to the heavens.

XXIII.

THE ISLAND OFF-SHORE

150.

—It is finished. All is left to be done.
How hard, therefore, it is to end, to die
In age, again and again, as one must do,
To read or pretend to read until it is
All memory, and then memory of memory
(All that which was a fire in the mind)
Except the moment of death, which is not
A moment in the mind and cannot be,
As the sun goes down to the north (*Selah*)

151.

And the island of which we both have heard
Is disclosed when the wind shifts off-shore
At evening and the mists are dispersed.
And the sun is "a fire in the mind,"
A figure of everything that can happen,
Now going down unextinguishable
Into the sea to the north and west of
The island (Catalina), never to return,
So slowly that we look away—indifferent—

152.

From the grand catastrophe on the horizon
Toward one another, our backs to the gigantic
Sun as it sinks down in silence . . .
And then, again, look out at ocean breathing,
As it does at evening, the long breaths
Of a body when it intends repose,
To see ("How changed! How fallen!") the world on fire,
Everything that can happen. —And this too
Is sunlight and the purpose of the sun.

153.

Then we look at one another to judge the distance
Between us, bearing with great care—patiently—
Like new glass—not light but the light of the eye,
Invisible to others ("What are they doing?
What?" they ask), that makes visible all things.
In our opinion, the glassy state is a fourth
State added to the water, air, and earth.
Not that there is another world experience
Does not know, but that experience is precisely

154.

(Fire in the mind) the other world experience
Does not know. And it is sanity to go
On where there is a purpose, but no end.
The end is the destination of the Jews
And it thunders over the farmer, Jerusalem.
In the end, all the pilgrims lay down their glass.
They have brought the world to mind, and sit
Together on a bed's edge and tell true stories
About the world. The gods listen and believe.

155.

Of what do the weeping birds descant at dawn
When the wind shifts off-shore and the island
Appears to the man and woman who listen,
Like souls that are alone, tired to death
Of love? "What do they sing?" she asks. "And what
Has love to do with it?" *There is no end,*
Unless the god throw down the smoking thunder-
Bolt and by that ruin make conclusion
—God of the waste places, land or ocean.

SELAH

Three

THE SNOWFALL

non me carminibus vincet nec Thracius Orpheus
Not even Thracian Orpheus shall vanquish me in song
Virgil, *Eclogue* IV

The Snowfall

(Oct. 23, 1939)

"Look. It has blue eyes!"

I.

At that time the boy spoke out loud, "O mother,
May I go out *now* to play in the garden?"
And the mother said: "Yes, dear. But you must take care.
In the garden are things that never were,
And also things that are no longer, alive.
And things destined to live, that are not yet
Alive even to this day. And all the memories
Of each of us, human and inhuman. But take greatest
Care for the things that are coming to be
And passing away. *They are fatal to the mind.*
In any case (said the mother), I think it's
Going to snow." —And then the boy went out
To play in the garden. And it was so.

II.

That morning the aeroplanes sailed against
The sky, their klaxons sounding. And the whole weight
Of the world rested, like a single word,
On the heel of the hand that played the horn
Of the wind. The philosophic oak had considered
The garden since 1932—the year I was born:
"There are still songs to be sung," he began.
"But master Orpheus is not the singer. Nor yet
Is Philomele—infanticide nightingale,
Her melody on the thorned nest—the song."
"Then, who *is* a master in America?" I ask.
"Who has blue eyes?" the oak replies. "The greatest
Poet is a hammer on the iron rail

III.

Of the universe!" A cloud came up. It was
Going to snow for the last time, October
1939. Out of the cloud fell down an infant
Snowflake. Though but new born, it spoke to me
(A voice of another kind!): *"My name is destiny."*
Thus speech will follow after other speech
To the human end. The sky darkens. The horn
Of the wind is heard. Over the crib of the
New-born word the oak tree utters its prophecy
In many voices confusedly. And from afar
The universe resounds like a hammered rail.
—All that day the silent snows poured down secrecy,
The poet's burden, on the cooling garden.

IV.

How to live on? The dead things and the living
Thing turn as they fall in the autumn garden.
The plumed seed, the prophetic leaf torn from
Oak, and the last worm turning on the air,
Turn also in mind. But the coldest elements,
The light in wires and the driven snow, are hurled
Level with our flesh to their destination
In the heart from the beginning of the world!
What did the infant snowflake feel in its cloud,
Falling and rising above America,
Among the first of its kind on a dark day
At the beginning of a long winter of snow?
It was only "getting to know" its kind;

V.

It had no knowledge of our inverted trees
Or the cooling ashes of our autumn gardens;
Nor had it looked upon our earth which is
Its sky and destiny—nor on our sky,
The material body from which it came
By a sheer inclination of the elements.

Now Orpheus at his instrument has stopped
His breath. Something new has startled him. "So
Beautiful," he says. "*Another voice!*
This is the onset of imagined snow."
—Absorbed, now, in its work the moaning oak,
From out the mysterious well of its dark root
And the long labor of its "mighty heart,"

VI.

Gives warning of a greater art. Philomele,
The nightingale, leaning upon her thorn,
Looks up, rises from the limb of her lament
And seats herself on the throne of the weather.
"A voice," she says, "from the next room over."
Beneath her claw the orphan, on its bed
Of sod, stares at the cloud from which it came.
(No longer crystalline. It is now flame
In the low light of the autumn storm.)
It sees that the trees are not as they should be.
It notes the left hand of the wind breaking oak
Leaves one by one—between its index finger,
Marked by a moon-like scar, and the sexual tool

VII.

Of the thumb. An odor streams upon the air.
Perfume! Half sex, half rage of prophecy:
"*Many, of course, will die below.*" That said,
The infant snowflake goes to bed at noon
And the snow comes down in the garden,
Building secrecy until the crack of doom.
"It has blue eyes," we cried. "Look what is born
October 22, 1939, the beginning of time."
—Now, in a room, at whatever distance from
The beginning of time, my hands are laid
Upon an instrument to make some music.
The score is open, today the garden page,
And there is silence in the heavens half an hour.

VIII.

Silence I will always remember! (Age
Changes nothing.) A silence of which to tell.
Silence like the ease after a long tale,
Ease of a mind that need not further go,
A mind that is at rest, its road gone over,
In the hour before dawn after a long
Night of snow. —The pastoral is restored!
As it was in the beginning of the garden:
Pathless innocence, shadowless loves,
Elemental hunger, the haunting of wolves.
Upon my hands, my hands intending music,
Other hands are laid from the next room over,
Other hands, stopping the play without a word.

IX.

A left hand covers my left and all its powers.
Another right my right with the scarred index finger
Covers over, in a mansion of numberless rooms
Each for a moment silent under the same snow.
Thus, a greater solitude by its grace bestows
(O the restraining hands!) upon the lesser
Solitude a deeper tone. And then descends,
Hand over hand without a word, the stair
Of silence, one tone at a time alone
To the beginning of time, October, 1939.
And there she is singing the elements,
The snow hand playing the snow part: pathless
Innocence, shadowless loves, elemental hunger

X.

And a distant hammer in the heart. Orpheus
Stares at the snowfield *with nothing to say.*
Philomele, enthroned, is looking another way.
The oak, never at a loss for words, speaks prophecy:
"We have reached," he murmurs, "the garden of silence,
America of light alone. I hear a distant

Hammer sound the iron rail of the heart
To find it true, or break it along the fault.
In a birth room, far away, the people shout
'A Master is born in America. *Our Voice.*
The fingers of its hands are white as snow:
The left hand, with all its powers, the right with
The scarred index finger. It has blue eyes. Rejoice!'

XI.

Woe to the nation that *awaits* a prophecy
That has come true." —Insistently, therefore,
The mind turns and returns on its own lines:
"Inasmuch as I have seen the winter weather,
And inasmuch as I have heard on a day
The wind utter a single word, and inasmuch
As I remember the mother's warning which foretold
Another turning in the long afternoon of song
And in another season pale hands from the next
Room over stopped the play, and inasmuch as we
Have fallen from a cloud—the first that day—
And lie diminishing on the cooling sod
Still warm with the heat of summer, disturbed

XII.

And broken by the hoe, fallow—: *therefore,*
We are doomed to thought until the greater poet
Come a second time (the one whom I saw
Flame when I was young) and perish in
The winter sun." In the silence now of
Which I tell the birth cries still resound
Throughout America. "New orphan!" is still
The call. "So beautiful!" "A cosmic scandal!"
"An unforgivable divine surprise!" of which
The rumor is it will be fatal, whispered
Even by the oldest trees such as the oak
Considered wise and capable of prophecy.
So speech follows other speaking after all.

XIII.

"O Mother! Tell me. How should a man live?"
—Far, far away the mother in her grave
Forgets to turn. Nor does she raise her eyes.
The aeroplanes sail against the sky in silence.
No klaxon heard. The snow fills all the pathways
Of the universe. There are no open roads,
Even among the stars. Imagined storms extend
Their secrecy from the beginning of
The world until the end. Subjected to the wind
The snows descend upon the garden of the mind
(Now silent). The orphan in the air appears
And disappears in flames, saying his say
As infants do: "My name is destiny."

XIV.

Out of their haunting the wolves return,
The shadowless loves. And ancient forests
Murmur behind the garden walls. A distant
Hammer on an iron rail expounds the romance
Of innocence: the long delay of the sheltering
Tree. White hands have stopped the play forever
And a voice of another kind is the fashion
Of our destiny. Speak of it, householder,
When you are sitting in your room, whether in company
Or alone; and when you walk the public ways;
And when you lie in bed and sigh: —the story
Of the snows, and of the greater poet,
Master of secrecy, who has blue eyes.

XV.

Now the mother speaks to me from above,
As the song of a hidden bird in the
Spring of the year is an omen of love:
"Can you hear me, Allen? Go out with a spade
To the garden, where things are coming to be
And passing away. Plant very young trees

Of the slow-growing kinds. And then endure
The long delay of the sheltering tree.
But when, at last, they crowd into a shade
Sit down in your kingdom—promised and made.''
—Thus, in my 60th year, a skater turns back
Across the thundering ice-roads of the winter lake
He wanders over, urgent to tell, feeding his snow
Hunger, how a snowflake fell in October.

Four

WHOEVER BUILDS

Unless the Lord builds the house,
its builders will have laboured in vain.

Whoever Builds

1.

Whoever builds puts himself in service to materials
And becomes subject to the laws of materials.
Therefore, whoever builds of earth becomes subject
To the laws of earth. And whoever builds
Of air becomes subject to the laws of air.
But whoever builds of the matter of water
Becomes subject to the laws of water,
And subject also to the laws of air
That build the house of the wind on the foundation
Of water, and subject also to the laws
Of earth that bind water and all its creatures,
Hold the water in—and make it a world.
And whoever builds of fire, whether man
Or woman, becomes subject to the laws
Of fire, older than the laws of earth
Or air or the water. —Do not dissemble
The true state of affairs *which is known*!

2.

At dawn each man and woman washes the body
That is given in a basin of white stone.
The light, reflected from the surface of the
Water onto the white wall of the bath,
Makes an ocean entirely of light: profound,
Transparent, fiery bright, under wind,
The best thing of all to see! —What then?
What is our work on that ocean of light?
What ports of call to be obtained? What destination?
What stories told among the sailors on the docks,
Or among the children of the town in the foothills
Where the steep road rises toward the mountain
And we sit down at midday to recruit
Our spirits for the climb? Or, in the bed
Of love at evening, amid the snows half-
Way to the top, tell stories before sleep,

The last thing? —On the top of the mountain
Dwell the gods, men and women lost in thought:
Lost, lost and alone in the general air
Without day or night, watched over by the
Watchman of the mountain. Below the gods,
The seasons begin and the one particular
Night hovers and sleeps. Within that night
I see, far off, the region of our dawn
In which we wake, bathe in the bright water,
And take our pleasure in the raking light.
Among the nights are nights that I remember,
And also nights that I do not remember.
Among nights that I remember are lesser
Nights and greater nights. Among the greater nights
I remember, in especial, *one white night*
On the mountain of time forty years ago.

That night I went out on the mountain path
Because a fire was in my head. Looking back
I saw the house go up in flames behind me.
And by that fire—oldest of the elements—
I saw within its light the disappointment
Of the children when the story ends. (It is
Easy to fall out of the mountain of time
In the dark at the hour before dawn.)
—That night there was no wind. The silver moonlight
Had not yet come down the stair. But soon enough
She raised a leg to give the old codger (the watch-
Man, her ancient lover) a chance at her ragged
Genital, etc., etc. (He has enough sperm
In him *still* to re-populate Chicago!)
Afterwards, she bathed her breasts in the sky-
Fallen spring (where the horse of the god stumbled),
And ran down the mountain with the other girls
While light showered refreshment on their pastels

5.

From beyond the stars. When, however, she stepped
One step lower than the moon, everything went
Grey on the rocky upland path at my feet.
Away to the north and east the risen moon,
From its stone, poured down the color
Of stone—the stony-grey of very great
Age which takes away names—upon the grasses
Upright, or lodged where an animal rested,
A dog (let us say) fallen from the moon.
And the green snake in the grass is gray
And the stones scattered on the path, like names
Thrown down in desperation by other climbers
As the sun rose and ascent became more difficult.
And the moonlight says to me, "What a disgrace
You are, fat man! Take this rod." And she says,
Tapping her left foot, *"I will not kiss you!"*
Then in her veils (not now pastel), she dances
Off, and her girl friends do likewise. —But I

6.

Saw the poet's vision (a night *remembered!*)
In the mountain of time: How that by gods
The world was made and *is without alternative
Made*. How they labor building up and ruining
The Great Work of Time with the gigantic
Instruments of their art—killing and quickening
In accord with the laws of materials
The use of which they know. That night, among
The upland grasses, all things and creatures
Spoke for the last time of the materials
And of the laws of materials as they
Are known to the gods until the silver moonlight
Came down the stair. For things are known because
Of the laws they utter night and day. Thereof
Whoever builds, the poet first of all,
Does makes his song. "Build up" (the poet sings)
"The house of water that the earth holds in

With wind whitening the waves. And on the hearth
Of it is fire—older than all things—older
Also than the gods who labor like men
And women (lost and alone, killing and quickening
In their reverie) who never kiss.

7.

For resistance is divine and knowledge of
Resistance is divine and part of the mastery,
As the wood resists the adze when the shipwright
Takes off the curl in short light strokes with a
Strong hand and the smiling iron keeps true
To the pilgrim keelson or the limber oar."
—What then of the mortal poet who must go up
The crooked track, perverse and obvious,
From stony Ascra to the mountain top?
By daylight the watchman's dog (which is fallen
From the moon) stands upon the stricken pathway
With fire in its eye preventing passage
Of the man or woman who has come up.
By night the lunar animal is at home.
Having raised his leg demurely, he stares me
Straight in the eye and pisses sacred fire
Against the mountain never to be quenched.
And the watchman whose dog it is says out loud,
"Take off your shoes, fat man. This is sacred ground."
And from within the flames the desecrated rock
Utters its law: "*Patience, patience. There is
Room for all in the house of victory.*"
Then, once again, I saw by the lights of fire
The ruins of the house I left behind
And the gigantic shadows which the gods,
Laborious, cast in their dream as they drag
Their irons among the ashes where sacred fire
Burns all things and creatures—and burns them up.

8.

Taking the rod in hand I entered on the struggle
With materials, or the shadows of materials,
Where the moon-dog held me on the mountain.
At dawn the shadow of earth stepped forward
From the other ashen shadows, hooked her right
Foot behind my left knee, and by a trick
Threw me out of the mountain of time
Into the dark. I lay where I fell down
Until noon, as if dead. But in the afternoon
The rains returned with the times and seasons,
And the fury of the wind with rain in it.
I am hopelessly in love with wind and rain
And with the voices of the wind and rain
And my own among them as among friends
And lovers. Yet it is not the voices of
Friends and lovers I love, for it is not lawful
To love voices, but the wind with rain in it
Repeating voices and my own among the rest.
Amid the rains of afternoon and the first
Watches of the night I slept sound, until
Aroused as I think now by the bright shadows
Of the seraphim when the rain stops and
The dark clouds flee away before the fires
Of dawn. *But the moon-dog's eyes burn on
Into the dawn-light.* Not eyes precisely,
But the victor's dream of eyes that look
At you, look long and hard as the light rises,
Then fade, toward noon, and look away,
Weary, lost, or subject to another cry.

9.

—Near the end of a long life, guilt accrues
(The wear, the wearing out, the darkest weathering).
And as the guilt accrues so also does the
Passion for a trial increase, *and judgement.*
But memory is witness, and the memories
Fall like water—like an iron fountain of

Bright water that has reached its highest point
Up there where the most light is in it
And falls back (drawn down by the weight of light)
Through windy air into successive basins
Each one heavier with swags of iron fruit
And crowded with more faces, less and less
Human, entirely iron, until the last basin
Which is boundless (*the love of love is a*
Great vocation) where all is lost, memory
Falling always with less light in it.

10.

"—That *something* did happen in fact at midnight
Before the rising of the moon is not
Contested. At the radio station, the technician
Who relieves me arrived exactly on time
Through a door that is usually locked
From the inside. I was startled because
I did not hear her customary signal
By rapping on the glass or calling out
To me, the solitary operator.
She arrived without my knowing she did
Through a door that is usually locked.
What Houdini, or other materialist Jew
With what key brought her across the impassible
Threshold to hang up a cloth coat with her
Purse still in the pocket like a flayed
Skin, the heart still beating and the excruciated
Face, still recognizable, putting its question?
Who but I, in this solitary place,
Could have stolen her purse? —To conclude
Otherwise would be a disaster for America."

11.

—At the water's edge among the reeds
The *malades* of Bethesda say in chorus,
The voice of each and the voice of all the same:
"Do not tell us, poet, about love or about

Suffering. *Tell us how the world was made.*
Tell us the secrets of the god who moves
Upon the water and we will die happy."
But the poet says this to the *malades*
Of Bethesda: "Listen! No one dies happy.
Whoever intends to build and does build,
Man or woman, servants of materials,
Stands first in the morning light thoroughly washed,
With the right clothes on, among lawful purities
And sacred things, *enduring patiently* the signals
That come ceaselessly to light and are known.
O you *malades* of Bethesda! No other
Act or practice of mind, no other inclination,
Could possibly effect the happiness
Of any person—no bending down or ex-
Altation, no quiet amid darkened rooms,
Nor fire when the mind leads on its seraphim
From ridge to ridge and takes the ancient trees
For its dwelling, and the houses of men
And women, and their bodies, and their souls."

12.

—At once, to the splendid city of water,
Winds, and shaken earth, the colors return.
On the path as we walk from the city, hand in hand,
Through the flowery meadows bordering upon
The cliff where the ocean surges and keeps
A Luna moth with the eyes of a person
And bright green wings, like quaking Aspen leaves
In June with wind in them, rests on the torn
Sack of its cocoon shuddering from the hard
Work of getting out. At the same time, exactly,
A wind of the world rises (as may happen
At that hour) from the grasses where it has
Slept since dawn and crosses the meadow path.
The leaves of the Aspen and young cottonwoods
Begin to shake in the wind, and the wings
Also of the great moth begin to shake
To be like the Aspen. Then there are only leaves.

For the great Luna moth has disappeared
Among them, being without distinction.
And we walk on at noon without a shadow
Into the nights and days of the June meadow.

Elle est retrouvée!
—Quoi?—l'Éternité.
C'est la mer mêlée
   Au soleil.

Five

JUNE, JUNE

June, June

What are the sounds that crowd the path
And linger above the unmown field?
Do you hear? —The winds of heaven are talking
In the language of the heart. "June, June,"
They say. "June. The lilacs are gone."

Wonderful things are weary of me:
The groaning meteors on the August road;
The pressed grasses where the great dog
Lay, that is fallen from the moon;
The heart that speaks in tongues, "June" and "June."

The snows are asleep in their treasuries,
With crossed feet. They are not yet thought.
At evening we see the ferry depart
Northeastward, at the appointed time,
Into the night and oncoming storm.

The ferry crosses from shore to shore
And disappears into the dark.
The grasses speak louder, "June, June."
The man and woman at the rail
Say to one another, "Who *could* have thought

What is spoken in the language of the heart!"
In the dark the ferry arrives
At the other shore. —And the snow?
The snows have come a long way, afoot,
And still have a long way to go.

Notes

The quotations from Rimbaud, in the presentation at the beginning of this book and at the end of the poem called "Whoever Builds," are from *Une Saison en Enfer*, respectively the "Adieu" and the "Delires" sections.

The epigraph to "The Philosopher's Window" is the last line of Mallarmé's "Brise Marine." The epigraph of "Whoever Builds" is of course from Psalm 127 of the biblical Book of Psalms. Virgil's fourth *Eclogue*, a line from which is translated at the beginning of "The Snowfall," proclaims the birth of a redemptive child.

"The Great Work Farm Elegy" honors the author's nephew, David Grossman, a man of noble character who died of AIDS. He is one of the dead children in blue—the one who questions the speaker. In the poem, an old man who has exhausted all other means of explanation undertakes by poetic means to speak of the *great work*. The story he tells begins with an account of the decline of the world—and, then, a knock on the door.

Children have come with questions. And the speaker labors at the fundamental reply—a life or death explanation—which he addresses to the questions of the children ("What did you mean? What!"). Early life and the end of life meet in the meadows and hayfields of "The Great Work Farm Elegy," where the work of early life is the building (under the tutelage of God and the farmer of earth) of the "golden house" (on the model of Adam's House in Paradise) and the work of the end of life is the singing of "The Song of the Constant Nymph" (which brings to mind the first hours of the world, before time began).

The poem of explanation is finally also the poem of the myth of explanation—the blank page, the page made blank by rain, which each person of whom an explanation is demanded (that is to say, *each person*) addresses and on which he or she inscribes "the long letter of mind" which she does or does not send, but which is in any case received—in any case blank.

In "The Philosopher's Window," a boy becomes a bird. This story, and much else in the poem, was brought to mind by Steven Feld's book, *Sound and Sentiment: Birds, Weeping, Poetics, and Song in Kaluli Expression* (1982).

Isambard Kingdom Brunel (1806-59) was a great British civil engineer. One of Brunel's first independent designs was for a suspension bridge across the river Avon at Bristol, which was however left incomplete during his life owing to lack of funds. After his death the bridge was erected, in accordance with his designs, by members of his profession. Adjacent to the bridge is a tower at the top of which is a rotating *camera obscura* for the viewing of the bridge, and the sublime gorge of Avon, and the adjacent moors. "Brunel's greatest fame was obtained in the construction of ocean-going steamships of dimensions larger than any previously known. . . . [His] crowning effort in shipbuilding was the design of the *Great Eastern*, the largest steamship yet built. . . . The work was begun in December 1853, and the *Great Eastern* entered the water on 31 January 1858. The delays and casualties attending her launch must be attributed to the novel and gigantic character of the undertaking and the imperfect calculations then applied to the problems of friction. . . . [Brunel] was present on 5 September 1859, at the trial of the engines, the day before the *Great Eastern* left the Thames. Ten days later he died. . . ." (*Dictionary of National Biography*)

The "Garden of Weeping Birds" is to be found in a well-known Sufi narrative of great force and beauty.

New Directions Paperbooks—A Partial Listing

For complete listing request free catalog from
New Directions, 80 Eighth Avenue, New York 10011   †Bilingual

Big Sur & The Oranges. NDP161.
The Colossus of Maroussi. NDP75.
A Devil in Paradise. NDP765.
Into the Heart of Life. NDP728.
The Smile at the Foot of the Ladder. NDP386.
Y. Mishima, Confessions of a Mask. NDP253.
Death in Midsummer. NDP215.
Frédéric Mistral, The Memoirs. NDP632.
Eugenio Montale, It Depends.† NDP507.
Selected Poems.† NDP193.
Paul Morand, Fancy Goods/Open All Night. NDP567.
Vladimir Nabokov, Nikolai Gogol. NDP78.
Laughter in the Dark. NDP729.
The Real Life of Sebastian Knight. NDP432.
P. Neruda, The Captain's Verses.† NDP345.
Residence on Earth.† NDP340.
Fully Empowered. NDP792.
New Directions in Prose & Poetry (Anthology).
Available from #17 forward to #55.
Robert Nichols, Arrival. NDP437.
Exile. NDP485.
J. F. Nims, The Six-Cornered Snowflake. NDP700.
Charles Olson, Selected Writings. NDP231.
Toby Olson, The Life of Jesus. NDP417.
George Oppen, Collected Poems. NDP418.
István Örkeny, The Flower Show/
The Toth Family. NDP536.
Wilfred Owen, Collected Poems. NDP210.
José Emilio Pacheco, Battles in the Desert. NDP637.
Selected Poems.† NDP638.
Nicanor Parra, Antipoems: New & Selected. NDP603.
Boris Pasternak, Safe Conduct. NDP77.
Kenneth Patchen, Because It Is. NDP83.
Collected Poems. NDP284.
Selected Poems. NDP160.
Ota Pavel, How I Came to Know Fish. NDP713.
Octavio Paz, Collected Poems. NDP719.
Configurations.† NDP303.
A Draft of Shadows.† NDP489.
Selected Poems. NDP574.
Sunstone.† NDP735.
A Tree Within.† NDP661.
St. John Perse, Selected Poems.† NDP545.
Ezra Pound, ABC of Reading. NDP89.
Confucius. NDP285.
Confucius to Cummings. (Anth.) NDP126.
Diptych Rome-London. NDP783.
A Draft of XXX Cantos. NDP690.
Elektra. NDP683.
Guide to Kulchur. NDP257.
Literary Essays. NDP250.
Personae. NDP697.
Selected Cantos. NDP304.
Selected Poems. NDP66.
The Spirit of Romance. NDP266.
Eça de Queiroz, Ilustrious House of Ramires. NDP785.
Raymond Queneau, The Blue Flowers. NDP595.
Exercises in Style. NDP513.
Mary de Rachewiltz, Ezra Pound. NDP405.
Raja Rao, Kanthapura. NDP224.
Herbert Read, The Green Child. NDP208.
P. Reverdy, Selected Poems.† NDP346.
Kenneth Rexroth, An Autobiographical Novel. NDP725.
Classics Revisited. NDP621.
More Classics Revisited. NDP668.
Flower Wreath Hill. NDP724.
100 Poems from the Chinese. NDP192.
100 Poems from the Japanese.† NDP147.
Selected Poems. NDP581.
Women Poets of China. NDP528.
Women Poets of Japan. NDP527.
Rainer Maria Rilke, Poems from
The Book of Hours. NDP408.
Possibility of Being. (Poems). NDP436.
Where Silence Reigns. (Prose). NDP464.
Arthur Rimbaud. Illuminations.† NDP56.
Season in Hell & Drunken Boat.† NDP97.
Edouard Roditi, Delights of Turkey. NDP445.

Jerome Rothenberg, Khurbn. NDP679.
The Lorca Variations. NDP771.
Nayantara Sahgal, Rich Like Us. NDP665.
Ihara Saikaku, The Life of an Amorous Woman. NDP270.
St. John of the Cross, Poems.† NDP341.
W. Saroyan, Fresno Stories. NDP793.
Jean-Paul Sartre, Nausea. NDP82.
The Wall (Intimacy). NDP272.
P. D. Scott, Crossing Borders. NDP796.
Listening to the Candle. NDP747.
Delmore Schwartz, Selected Poems. NDP241.
In Dreams Begin Responsibilities. NDP454.
Hasan Shah, The Dancing Girl. NDP777.
K. Shiraishi, Seasons of Sacred Lust. NDP453.
Stevie Smith, Collected Poems. NDP562.
Novel on Yellow Paper. NDP778.
Gary Snyder, The Back Country. NDP249.
The Real Work. NDP499.
Turtle Island. NDP381.
Muriel Spark, The Comforters. NDP796.
The Driver's Seat. NDP786.
The Public Image. NDP767.
Enid Starkie, Rimbaud. NDP254.
Stendhal, Three Italian Chronicles. NDP704.
Antonio Tabucchi, Indian Nocturne. NDP666.
Nathaniel Tarn, Lyrics . . . Bride of God. NDP391.
Dylan Thomas, Adventures in Skin Trade. NDP183.
A Child's Christmas in Wales. NDP181.
Collected Poems 1934–1952. NDP316.
Collected Stories. NDP626.
Portrait of the Artist as a Young Dog. NDP51.
Quite Early One Morning. NDP90.
Under Milk Wood. NDP73.
Tian Wen: A Chinese Book of Origins. NDP624.
Uwe Timm, The Snake Tree. NDP686.
Lionel Trilling, E. M. Forster. NDP189.
Tu Fu, Selected Poems. NDP675.
N. Tucci, The Rain Came Last. NDP688.
Paul Valéry, Selected Writings.† NDP184.
Elio Vittorini, A Vittorini Omnibus. NDP366.
Rosmarie Waldrop, A Key into the Language of America.
NDP798.
Robert Penn Warren, At Heaven's Gate. NDP588.
Eliot Weinberger, Outside Stories. NDP751.
Nathanael West, Miss Lonelyhearts &
Day of the Locust. NDP125.
J. Wheelwright, Collected Poems. NDP544.
Tennessee Williams, Baby Doll. NDP714.
Cat on a Hot Tin Roof. NDP398.
Collected Stories. NDP784.
The Glass Menagerie. NDP218.
Hard Candy. NDP225.
A Lovely Sunday for Creve Coeur. NDP497.
One Arm & Other Stories. NDP237.
Red Devil Battery Sign. NDP650.
The Roman Spring of Mrs. Stone. NDP770.
A Streetcar Named Desire. NDP501.
Sweet Bird of Youth. NDP409.
Twenty-Seven Wagons Full of Cotton. NDP217.
Vieux Carre. NDP482.
William Carlos Williams.
Asphodel. NDP794.
The Autobiography. NDP223.
Collected Poems: Vol. I. NDP730.
Collected Poems: Vol. II. NDP731.
The Doctor Stories. NDP585.
Imaginations. NDP329.
In The American Grain. NDP53.
In The Money. NDP240.
Paterson. Complete. NDP152.
Pictures from Brueghel. NDP118.
Selected Poems (new ed.). NDP602.
White Mule. NDP226.
Wisdom Books:
St. Francis. NDP477; Taoists. NDP509;
Wisdom of the Desert. NDP295; Zen Masters.
NDP415.

For complete listing request free catalog from
New Directions, 80 Eighth Avenue, New York 10011   †Bilingual